Doing Battle with the Names of God

Spiritual Warfare for the Reluctant Warrior

Catrina J. Sparkman

ISBN 13: 978-1-949958-12-06

THE
IRONER'S
PRESS

The Doing Business with God Series
Presents:

Doing Battle with the Names of God
Spiritual Warfare for the Reluctant Warrior

Catrina J. Sparkman

Doing Battle with the Names of God
Copyright © 2016 Catrina J. Sparkman
Published by The Ironer's Press
Softcover edition ISBN 13: 978-1-949958-12-06

THE
IRONER'S
PRESS

All rights reserved. No part of this book may be reproduced, stored in whole or in part or transmitted in any form by any means, without prior written permission from the publisher, except in the case of brief quotations embodied in articles for review. Nor can this book be circulated in any form of binding or cover other than that in which it is published. All Bible Scriptures taken from the following translations: New International Standard Version, God's Word Translation, English Standard Version, and The King James Version.

DEDICATION

For Lil who inspired me to write this

Check out these other great titles by Catrina J. Sparkman

Non Fiction

Doing Business with God: An Everyday Guide to Prayer and Journaling

Intimacy the Beginning of Authority

Divine Revelation for a Twitter Generation: Growing in the Prophetic

Intercession the Heartbeat of God

The Fourth Watch: A Watch For Prophets, Warriors, Intercessors & Lovesick Believers

Fiction

Passing Through Water

Opening the Floodgates

The Fire This Time

TABLE OF CONTENTS

Author's Note: i

Introduction: **Me A Solider in the Army? 1**

Chapter 1: **Prince of Peace, Man of War 5**

Chapter 2: **Goliath 13**

Chapter 3: **The Philistines Kidnap Grandma 23**

Chapter 4: **The Philistines Kill Batman 27**

Chapter 5: **The Philistines Capture the Ark 35**

Chapter 6: **A Technologically Superior Enemy 41**

Chapter 7: **Saul Written Out of History 49**

Chapter 8: **Then Came David 57**

Chapter 9: **Twenty Names to Use in Battle 71**

Epilogue: **An Invitation to the Family of God 90**

About the Author **93**

AUTHOR'S NOTE

First and foremost, I want to take a moment to thank you for purchasing your copy of, *Doing Battle with the Names of God: Spiritual Warfare for the Reluctant Warrior*. In a time in our society when we are inundated by multiple forms of entertainment, many of which we can have at a touch of a button, thank you for taking time out of your busy life to read this book.

This book is a part of a suite of books in a series I call, *Doing Business with God*. Which also, by the way, happens to the title of my first published book. The purpose of the books in the Doing Business with God series, is to teach modern day believers how to walk in authority while working in concert with Heaven to bring the will of God into Earth. Whew, that's a mouthful, I know, but I desperately believe this is one of the primary reasons we've been put on this planet. As you can probably guess, knowing how to confidently engage in spiritual warfare is a great tool to have in your arsenal if you are going to be about the business of bringing God's government into the Earth.

I decided to write *Doing Battle with the Names of God Spiritual Warfare for the Reluctant Warrior* because in the area of spiritual warfare, I've discovered two common misconceptions operating among modern day believers. First, as Christians, we have the tendency to think that we have to reach the status of super- Christian, before we can engage in the big stuff like, like doing battle with the forces of darkness. Secondly, we think we cannot even begin to consider this first thing if we don't lead sinless, perfect lives.

The reality is that we all sin and fall short of the glory of God. God doesn't give out super suits. Well, actually, I'll retract that last statement because He absolutely does give out superhero suits. It's called the Ephesian 6 Armor of Christ. But here's the thing folks, He treats all of His children the same. We all get that same super suit. All we have to do is put it on. Wrong thinking about themselves as it relates to the spiritual realms is the number one reason modern day believers don't take authority over their cities, homes, schools, neighborhoods and communities. *Doing Battle with the Names of God* is written to be a basic spiritual warfare primer that every believer, from the youngest child to the oldest adult can use. And even if you are not a beginner, even if you do battle with the big boys, the dark, scary forces of Satan every day, there are some foundational truths here in this book that will help you become more effective in understanding the how and the why behind what you do.

Like some of my other books in the *Doing Business with God* series, I've included random spaces throughout the physical edition of this book where you can take a moment to *Selah*. Selah is a word that is used 74 times in scripture. Sometimes the psalmist will tell us to Selah after a particular verse. The word simply means to pause and think on that. If you are reading the Kindle edition or listening to the audio version of this book feel free to use a dedicated study journal for those Selah moments.

I've also included a glossary of terms at the end of this book. This particular glossary is a list of twenty names of God. It includes insight on how and when to use each of these names during your time of worship and intercession. You don't want to skip over this part of the book. After I convince you of your right to war, the practical application of how to apply this teaching to your own life will be found in the glossary section of this book.

So without further ado it is my great pleasure to present to you, *Doing Battle with the Names of God: Spiritual Warfare for the Reluctant Warrior*. Blessings to you my friend, and may you learn to treasure every part of the journey, even the crooked places that the Master comes to make straight.

Sincerely,

Catrina J. Sparkman

Doing Battle with the Names of God

Spiritual Warfare for the Reluctant Warrior

I'm a soldier in the army of the Lord!
BOOM
I thought that was just a Song!

INTRODUCTION

ME A SOLIDER IN THE ARMY?

We all remember the song we sang at Bible camp, "I'm a Solider in the Army of the Lord! I'm a Solider in the Army!" It had a rousing beat, was often accompanied by foot stomps, and hand claps, and perhaps there was even an organist playing in the background. The song leader would throw out a couple of made up verses on the fly like, "I believe I'll thank him!" To which the congregation would reply, "In the army of the Lord!" We sang this song loud, and we sang it proud, but we didn't actually think that we were in a real army, with actually bullets, weapons, and Heaven forbid . . . casualties.

> Love, peace and joy in the kingdom are all birthrights of believers but there is another side of the coin. There is also war.

The old saints sang that song for a reason. They knew and understood what the next generation of believers hadn't quite figured out yet. That there is a very real battle raging in the heavenly realms. A battle that everyone who professes Jesus as their Lord and Savior will one day ultimately have to join. This book was written for every Christian who ever came into the kingdom of God and experienced a culture shock. For those that didn't know they had to fight, and for those who figured, 'Yeah, I expected a fight, I just didn't know the battle would be this fierce.' This book is for every battle-weary believer who has put down their sword. It's for every Christian that came to Christ and thought there would be love, peace, and joy in the kingdom. All of that is true. All of that is the birthright of the believer. But there is another side of that coin–there is also war.

During the course of this study we will be focusing on the nation of Israel, the offspring of one very faithful man who believed God. Israel was a thriving farming community of ordinary people who had to learn how to fight. These people were not warriors. They were everyday folks who were chosen by God. And it was the call of God on their lives that made them a target to the demonic forces of this world that knew that the Christ King would one day enter the Earth through their family lineage.

In this study, we will also be looking at the life of David, Israel's most celebrated warrior king. Why you may ask? Because David fought his most critically acclaimed battle **before** he was formally trained as a solider. He was just a shepherd boy, an ordinary citizen in love with praising his Lord and King. By using the strategies and methods of David, you will see how you can gain similar victories over the spiritual giants in your own world.

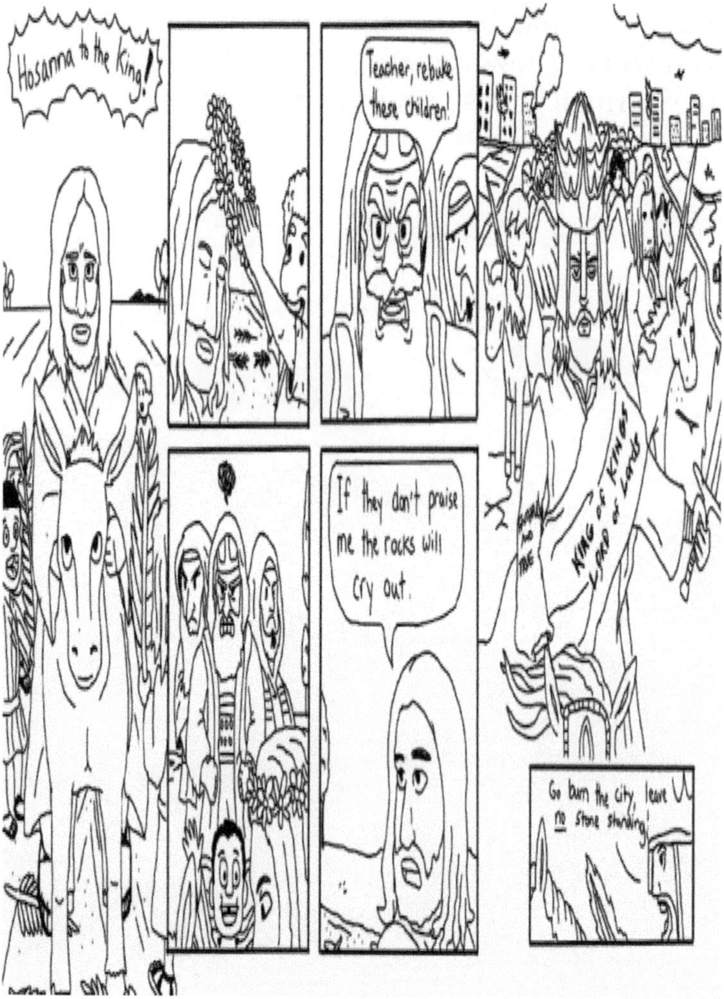
Hosanna to the King!
Teacher, rebuke these children!
If they don't praise me the rocks will cry out.
KING of KINGS
LORD of Lords
Go burn the city, leave NO stone standing!

CHAPTER ONE

PRINCE OF PEACE, MAN OF WAR

Warfare isn't always a popular topic in Christian circles. In fact, some of us feel like war and talk of war is downright demonic. After all, how can a God who tells us to turn the other cheek also tell us to fight? Simple, Jesus is called the Prince of Peace (Isaiah 9:6), yet He is also referred to as a Man of War (Exodus 15:3). The Jesus that we see on Palm Sunday riding meekly on the back of a donkey is not the same one we meet in Revelation who shall return with a sword in His mouth.
(Revelation 1:16, 19:15)

> Our multifaceted God can talk to us in His Word about both love and war, about both swords and cheeks because our battle should never be against people.

Seeing Jesus both as the Prince of Peace and a Man of War causes us to look at God through the lens of balance. Just like our Christian lives must be lived with balance. We must be bringers of His peace, but we must also not shrink back from war. Jesus speaking to His disciples said:

Peace I leave with you; my peace I give you. I do not give to you as the world gives. Do not let your hearts be troubled and do not be afraid.
John 14:27

Paul echoes Jesus' sentiment and follows behind saying:

For the kingdom of God is not a matter of eating and drinking, but of righteousness, peace, and joy in the Holy Spirit, because anyone who serves Christ in this way is pleasing to God and approved by men. Let us therefore make every effort to do what leads to peace and to mutual edification.
Romans 14: 17-19

Still there are many times in the Bible that God specifically told His people to make war on their enemies and to completely wipe them out. (See Deuteronomy 20: 16-17, Numbers 31:2 and 1 Samuel 15: 18). Now of course there are many debates about this, some argue that these instructions from God to fight and kill only apply to the Old Testament and that the Jesus, who told His disciples to turn the other cheek (Matthew 5:39) would never condone war or violence of any sort.

Yet, there is absolutely nothing in scripture that validates this concept of Jesus being a pacifist. Jesus said, "When you see me you have seen the Father" (John 14:9). He also said that, "I and the Father are one," (John 10:30). If God the Father is a Man of War, then you can be assured that Jesus is a Man of War also (Exodus 15:3). In fact, Jesus is the Commander of the Lord's Army that appeared to Joshua:

Now when Joshua was near Jericho, he looked up and saw a man standing in front of him with a drawn sword in his hand. Joshua went up to him and asked, "Are you for us or for our enemies?" "Neither," he replied, "but as commander of the army of the Lord I have now come." Then Joshua fell facedown to the ground in reverence, and asked him, "What message does my Lord have for his servant?" The commander of the Lord's Army replied, "Take off your sandals, for the place where you are standing is holy." And Joshua did so.
Joshua 5:13-15

Please note that this is not an angel. Joshua is speaking with the Pre-incarnated Christ. Jesus is revealing an aspect of His nature and personality to Joshua that the Israelites sorely need. All of the older generation, including the warriors, have died in the desert. Joshua is about to lead a very large group of untrained civilians into the already occupied Promised Land when only two people in the group have combat experience—Joshua and Caleb, the only elders among them left alive. Israel desperately needs the military expertise of the Commander of the Lord's Army right about now!

The first lesson that Joshua learns about the Commander of the Lord's Army is that He doesn't *work* for anyone. He is God. If Israel wants help from Him they must realize that both the battle and the victory belong to Him.

Joshua has the proper response. He falls to his face and worships. Joshua gets the message from Heaven loud and clear. This is God. Just as Daniel would later understand and be grieved by the antichrist spirit he saw in his vision. Daniel is disturbed because he said that the antichrist spirit was trying to make himself equal to the Commander of the Lord's Army. The reason that Daniel is so grieved in his spirit about this is because he knows that the Commander of the Lord's Army is God (Daniel 8:11).

Had the heavenly being that visited Joshua been merely an angel sent from God, even an archangel, the being never would have allowed Joshua to fall down and worship him. (See Daniel 8:17-18, Revelation 22:8-9.) Angels know all too well about the judgment that awaits anyone who would attempt to steal the Commander's glory. No, this is Jesus—the very Word spoken from the Father's mouth. He was present in the beginning as collaborator, in the creation process with both the Father and the Holy Spirit.

In the beginning was the Word, and the Word was with God, and the Word was God. He was with God without him nothing was made that has been made. In him was life, and that life was the light of all mankind. The light shines in the darkness, and the darkness has not overcome it.

John 1: 1-5

If God the Father, who does not change, tells His people to utterly consume their enemies, you can rest assured that Jesus said it too.

Ecclesiastes 3:8 tells us that there is a season for everything. War certainly is inevitable in the sin sick world that we live in. Had Hitler not been defeated in World War II, millions more Jews would have been killed and had the South not been defeated in the American Civil War, African Americans in this country might still be enslaved. This multifaceted God we serve can talk to us in His Word about both love and war, about both swords and cheeks because our battle should never be about or against people.

Finally, be strong in the Lord and in his mighty power. Put on the full armour of God, so that you can take your stand against the devil's schemes. For our struggle is not against flesh and blood, but against the rulers, against the authorities, against the powers of this dark world and against the spiritual forces of evil in the heavenly realms.

Ephesians 6:10-12

Paul, under the inspiration of the Holy Ghost gives us a glimpse into the unseen realms. He tells us who the target is. He says that our opponents are of the strong, dark, and wicked variety, but that they aren't made of flesh and blood. They are spiritual forces of evil that abide in unseen heavenly realms. So how in the world can we ever expect to overcome an enemy that we can't see? That Beloved, is the premise of this entire book. We will overcome the enemy of our souls by doing what Joshua did, and what Daniel did. We will employ the strategies of David because our help is in the Name of the Lord.

SELAH NOTES

Which one of you Israelite Cowards will Come up to fight me?!
...
Men, the King has promised abundant riches, his daughter's hand in marriage, and no taxes for the family of the man who will be brave enough to kill the Philistine giant.
Wait, no taxes? For how long?
Forever.
hm...
Nope, not worth it.

CHAPTER TWO

GOLIATH

Now the Philistines gathered their forces for war and assembled at Sokoh in Judah. They pitched camp at Ephes Dammim, between Sokoh and Azekah. Saul and the Israelites assembled and camped in the Valley of Elah and drew up their battle line to meet the Philistines. The Philistines occupied one hill and the Israelites another, with the valley between them. A champion named Goliath, who was from Gath, came out of the Philistine camp. His height was six cubits and a span. He had a bronze helmet on his head and wore a coat of scale armor of bronze weighing five thousand shekels; on his legs he wore bronze greaves, and a bronze javelin was slung on his back. His spear shaft was like a weaver's rod, and its iron point weighed six

> Although Goliath in this story is very real, he is also a metaphor for the enemy you can't possibly defeat on your own. This battle is not yours. You need the Lord.

hundred shekels. His shield bearer went ahead of him. Goliath stood and shouted to the ranks of Israel, "Why do you come out and line up for battle? Am I not a Philistine, and are you not the servants of Saul? Choose a man and have him come down to me. If he is able to fight and kill me, we will become your subjects; but if I overcome him and kill him, you will become our subjects and serve us." Then the Philistine said, "This day I defy the armies of Israel! Give me a man and let us fight each other." On hearing the Philistine's words, Saul and all the Israelites were dismayed and terrified.

1 Samuel 17: 1-11

We all know the story, right? It's the stuff that legends are made of. The Philistines come to attack Israel and they sent out their best warrior, Goliath. Goliath is over nine feet tall. He's got 5000 shekels of brass armor on his body— which is about the equivalent 125 pounds of metal. The tip of his spear alone weighs 15 pounds. His coat of armor is woven tightly like the scales of a fish. The garment allows him to be agile, to have freedom of movement, while at the same time remaining virtually in-destructible. This guy is a biblical version of the Terminator. He is impossible to kill and that is the whole point of the story. Although the giant in this story is very real, he is also a metaphor for the battle and the enemy that you cannot possibly defeat on your own. This battle is not yours. You need the Lord. Goliath comes out to the valley of Elah every day, bellowing curses at the top of his lungs. He mocks Israel. He mocks their God and he mocks Saul, their king.

The whole army of Israel is literally quaking in their boots. They aren't just afraid because Goliath is enormous, and strapped. Israel is afraid because Goliath represents a generational enemy. The Philistines are an ancient adversary that has vexed Israel throughout every generation. No matter how many times Israel fights the Philistines, they just keep coming back.

Have you ever had to fight a devil that just kept coming back? No matter how many times you knocked him down, he just got right back up and kept pursuing you? Perhaps you've had to deal with a reoccurring sickness, such as a genetic predisposition. Your mother fought it, your grandmother fought it. You bound and rebuked it in your generation, you plead the blood of Jesus — and for a time you had victory, but now all of a sudden, the doctors tell you that it's back.

The Philistines were a reoccurring cancer for Israel. Sometimes Israel found themselves on top of their enemy, and sometimes they were completely trampled underneath them. One might be prone to think that since Israel had fought this enemy many times before that they shouldn't have responded to Goliath with fear. Well, let me tell you, it's one thing to mount up for a battle you know without a shadow of a doubt that you're going to win. It's a whole nother story to fight a battle when you don't know what the outcome will be. When Goliath stood in the Valley of Elah, raining down curses on the children of Israel, it wasn't just a giant in the here and now that they had to contend with, it was history.

So, why would a nation who could retell the stories of a Pharaoh being drowned in the Red Sea and of their ancestors walking across that sea on dry ground not run to the battle? Surely every people group on the face of the Earth had heard what God had done for this nation, including the Philistines. Surely everyone knew that out of all the people groups of the Earth, Israel was God's favored son.

In the next few chapters I want to take some time and explore Israel's history. I want us to take a look at the parameters in place that would cause a nation with such a prophetically rich history to become afraid of their enemy.

But before I do that I want you to take a Selah moment—a pause and think about it moment. I want you to think about your own history. Is there something from your past that is presently threatening you? Can you name it? Can you identify it? Now I want you to take your attention off of the threat and think instead about the goodness of the Lord. Think about all the ways that God has shown Himself to you and your family.

SELAH NOTES

Abraham of Ur seeks an audience with you.
Abimelech
Husband, why is that man staring at me like that? He is creeping me out.
Even though you are close 90 You are still very lovely my dear. Just remember, if anybody asks you, for my sake, tell them you are my sister.
We are simple people, herdsmen, who just moved into the area. We ask permission to settle among you.
Sure, live among us. Wherever you like. Perhaps our people can intermarry.
You are as lovely as a desert flower. Do me a honor of becoming one of my wives.
But I'm already ma-
SWIPE!
SARAH!

CHAPTER THREE

THE PHILISTINES KIDNAP GRANDMA

Now Abraham moved on from there into the region of the Negev and lived between Kadesh and Shur. For a while he stayed in Gerar, and there Abraham said of his wife Sarah, "She is my sister." Then Abimelech king of Gerar sent for Sarah and took her. But God came to Abimelech in a dream one night and said to him, "You are as good as dead because of the woman you have taken; she is a married woman." Now Abimelech had not gone near her, so he said, "Lord, will you destroy an innocent nation? Did he not say to me, 'She is my sister,' and

> Sometimes we find ourselves at odds with systems and structures even people, and we can't figure out why or exactly *how* we got there. Sometimes we got there because God, Himself picked the fight.

didn't she also say, 'He is my brother'? I have done this with a clear conscience and clean hands." Then God said to him in the dream, *"Yes, I know you did this with a clear conscience, and so I have kept you from sinning against me. That is why I did not let you touch her. Now return the man's wife, for he is a prophet, and he will pray for you and you will live. But if you do not return her, you may be sure that you and all who belong to you will die."* Early the next morning Abimelech summoned all his officials, and when he told them all that had happened, they were very much afraid. Then Abimelech called Abraham in and said, *"What have you done to us? How have I wronged you that you have brought such great guilt upon me and my kingdom? You have done things to me that should never be done."* And Abimelech asked Abraham, *"What was your reason for doing this?"* Abraham replied, *"I said to myself, 'There is surely no fear of God in this place, and they will kill me because of my wife.' Besides, she really is my sister, the daughter of my father though not of my mother; and she became my wife. And when God had me wander from my father's household, I said to her, 'This is how you can show your love to me: Everywhere we go, say of me, "He is my brother."* Then Abimelech brought sheep and cattle and male and female slaves and gave them to Abraham, and he returned Sarah his wife to him. And Abimelech said, *"My land is before you; live wherever you like."* To Sarah he said, *"I am giving your brother a thousand shekels of silver. This is to cover the offense against you before all who are with you; you are completely vindicated."* Then Abraham prayed to God, and God healed Abimelech, his wife and his female slaves so they could have children *again, for the Lord had kept all the women in Abimelech's household from conceiving because of Abraham's wife Sarah.*

Genesis 20: 1-18

Long ago, before any of the Israelites where ever born, Abraham's wife Sarah was taken by the Philistine King. Perhaps you may remember Father Abraham? God called Abraham and his wife Sarah out of Ur and told him to get up, pack everything and move to a land that he had never heard of. God would give this land to them and their ancestors would possess it. But there are a few challenges that have to be overcome before the word of the Lord to Abraham can come to pass. Number one, Sarah, Abraham's wife is barren. Number two, Abraham is well past the age of ninety, himself. Number three, when they get to this patch of land in the middle of the desert, it's already inhabited by a whole lot of folk who don't acknowledge God or ascribe to His ways. I can hear Heaven laughing, because these are the perfect parameters for God to do a miracle.

God tells Abraham, "Don't pay any mind to these people you see roaming around here. The whole Earth is mine. I'm going to give you this land and I will make your ancestors as numerous as the sands on the seashore." God also tells Abraham, "Don't worry about your age or Sarah's infertility because there is absolutely nothing too hard for me."

Abimelech the Philistine king is one of the people who doesn't acknowledge the supremacy of God and who lives this land. He sees Sarah, Abraham's wife, and decides she is beautiful and that he should have her for himself. No doubt about it, for a senior citizen, Sarah is beautiful, but Abimelech is being demonically inspired. In the spirit realm Satan sees what's going on. God has set Abraham apart from all the people on Earth. Surely God has decided to use Abraham in His end time plan. Satan inspires Abraham to fear, and he inspires King Abimelech to lust after Abraham's wife. But God intervenes.

I don't know about you, but Abraham and Sarah's story inspires me. Their story helps me to understand that what God has for me, is for me. Even when I make a wrong turn in life—and trust me, I have made some wrong turns, God's ultimate purpose shall be fulfilled in my life. This excites me. It causes me to meet each new day with joy and expectancy instead of fear and despondency because God has the wherewithal to lead me out of this maze.

Now in Abimelech's defense, Abraham is afraid so he never gets around to telling Abimelech that Sarah is his wife. Abraham has observed these people in the short amount of time he has been living among them. There was something about the way the Philistines went about their day to day lives that told Abraham that these people where ruthless. Certainly not followers of the Living God. Abraham instructs Sarah to pay him a kindness and tell people that he is her brother. It wasn't a lie but it wasn't the whole truth either. For the nation of Israel's sake, for the Christ King that would come through that family line's sake, and for every person on the planet who would come into the Kingdom of God by receiving Jesus, thankfully God intervenes.

Now what we must keep in mind during this whole story is that Abraham is God's friend. Even when they are in the wrong, God is *always, always* very good to his friends. God appears to Abimelech in the middle of the night and says to him, "You're a dead man walking, buddy. That woman you took is another man's wife." God shuts up every womb in the Abimelech's house and threatens him with certain death. Abimelech apologizes profusely, pays Abraham generously, and from that moment on generational warfare is born between these two people groups.

I want you to know that when Goliath stood in the Valley of Elah raining down curses on the children of Israel, the Philistines had this historical data in their possession. The Philistines knew the story. They knew that the God of the Hebrews had made a distinction between the Hebrews and every other people group on the planet. They also knew that throughout history, the Living God had favored Israel. Through the oral storytelling traditions of the Philistine culture, each new generation would have more than likely inherited along with these stories, a deep seeded hatred for Israel. Everyone in the Valley of Elah that day knew that this thing between them was generational. But what they probably didn't know was that God was the one who had picked the fight.

Sometimes we find ourselves at odds with systems and structures and yes even people, and we can't figure out why or exactly *how* we got there. Sometimes we got there because God, Himself picked the fight. We can all agree that the Word of God is true, right? I mean, you probably wouldn't be reading this particular book if that wasn't a truism in your life. Anyways, here's where I'm going with this. The Holy Writ tells us that the steps of a righteous man are ordered by the Lord. And just in case you are a believer reading this and the enemy is looking over your shoulder right now whispering in your ear saying, "Well that doesn't apply to you, cause you're not holy and you aren't righteous."

Let me also remind you that the scripture also tells us that none of us are righteous. Not one. Our righteousness compared to that of God's is likened in the scripture to filthy menstrual rags (Isaiah 64:6). Yeah, that's some pretty gross stuff and it certainly won't do. Thank God for Jesus who is righteous. By His sacrifice, He made us righteous. His righteous was afforded unto us (1 Corinthians 1:30, Philippians 3:9).

So if the steps of the righteous man are ordered by the Lord, and we can now both agree that 1) they are, and 2) that righteous man is you. Can it also be true that the warfare that has come to your house, that it came from God too?

Could it be that God has picked this fight? I'm talking about the battle that you are currently in? Could it be that the situation that you think has come to utterly destroy you, to wipe you out, could it just be God inviting you out into the battlefield? Could it be that God is standing behind you, checking your form, guiding yours hands in the proper technique of how to draw back your bow and release your arrow? One thing is certain, if God has picked this fight, then no matter how it looks right now, you cannot lose because it is impossible for Him to lose. There is no failure in Him.

Samson, tell me the secret of your strength.
Please, I can't tell you that, girl. I'm Israel's Batman!
LATER...
Three times now, you've made a complete fool of me. How is this relationship ever going to work if you're not honest with me?
It's my hair, alright! I made a vow to the Lord to never cut it. He endows me with power! That's the secret to my strength.
Nice work Delilah.

CHAPTER FOUR

THE PHILISTINES KILL BATMAN

Sometime later, [Samson] fell in love with a woman in the Valley of Sorek whose name was Delilah. The rulers of the Philistines went to her and said, "See if you can lure him into showing you the secret of his great strength and how we can overpower him so we may tie him up and subdue him. Each one of us will give you eleven hundred shekels of silver." So Delilah said to Samson, "Tell me the secret of your great strength and how you can be tied up and subdued." Samson answered her, "If anyone ties me with seven fresh bowstrings that have not been dried, I'll become as weak as any other man." Then the rulers of the Philistines brought her seven fresh bowstrings that had not been dried, and she tied him with them. With men

> **Pray for good friends and godly relationships. The right people can propel you towards the future God has in store for you, but the wrong people can pervert and destroy your destiny.**

hidden in the room, she called to him, "Samson, the Philistines are upon you!" But he snapped the bowstrings as easily as a piece of string snaps when it comes close to a flame. So the secret of his strength was not discovered. Then Delilah said to Samson, "You have made a fool of me; you lied to me. Come now, tell me how you can be tied." He said, "If anyone ties me securely with new ropes that have never been used, I'll become as weak as any other man." So Delilah took new ropes and tied him with them. Then, with men hidden in the room, she called to him, "Samson, the Philistines are upon you!" But he snapped the ropes off his arms as if they were threads. Delilah then said to Samson, "All this time you have been making a fool of me and lying to me. Tell me how you can be tied." He replied, "If you weave the seven braids of my head into the fabric on the loom and tighten it with the pin, I'll become as weak as any other man." So while he was sleeping, Delilah took the seven braids of his head, wove them into the fabric and tightened it with the pin. Again she called to him, "Samson, the Philistines are upon you!" He awoke from his sleep and pulled up the pin and the loom, with the fabric.[15] Then she said to him, "How can you say, 'I love you,' when you won't confide in me? This is the third time you have made a fool of me and haven't told me the secret of your great strength." With such nagging she prodded him day after day until he was sick to death of it. So he told her everything. "No razor has ever been used on my head," he said, "because I have been a Nazirite dedicated to God from my mother's womb. If my head were shaved, my strength would leave me, and I would become as weak as any other man." When Delilah saw that he had told her everything, she sent word to the rulers of the Philistines, "Come back once more; he has told me everything." So the rulers of the Philistines returned with the silver in their hands. After putting him to sleep on her lap, she called for someone to shave off the seven braids of his hair, and so began to subdue him. And his strength left him. Then she called, "Samson, the Philistines are upon you!" He awoke from his sleep and thought, "I'll go out as before and shake myself free." But he did not know that the LORD had left him. Then the Philistines seized him, gouged out his eyes and took him down to Gaza. Binding him with bronze shackles, they set him to grinding grain in the prison. But the hair on his head began to grow again after it had been shaved. Now the rulers of the Philistines assembled to offer a great sacrifice to Dagon their god and to celebrate, saying, "Our god has delivered Samson, our enemy, into our hands." When the people saw him, they praised their god, saying, "Our god has delivered our enemy into our hands, the one who laid waste our land and multiplied our slain." While they were in high spirits, they shouted, "Bring out Samson to entertain us." So they called Samson out of the prison, and he performed for them. When they stood him among the pillars, Samson said to the servant who held his hand, "Put me where I can feel the pillars that support the temple, so that I may lean against them." Now the temple was crowded with men and women; all the rulers of the Philistines were there, and on the roof were about three thousand men and women watching Samson perform. Then Samson prayed to the LORD, "Sovereign LORD, remember me. Please, God, strengthen me just once more, and let me with one *blow get revenge on the Philistines for my two eyes." Then Samson reached toward the two central pillars on which the temple stood. Bracing himself against them, his right hand on the one and his left hand on the other, Samson said, "Let me die with the Philistines!" Then he pushed with all his might, and down came the temple on the rulers and all the people in it. Thus he killed many more when he died than while he lived. Then his brothers and his father's whole family went down to get him. They brought him back and buried him between Zorah and Eshtaol in the tomb of Manoah his father. He had led Israel twenty years.*

Judges 16: 4-31

    Many of us know the story of Samson. He was the closest thing to a superhero the Israelites had ever seen. Samson is probably the most famous, and certainly the most notorious judge to rule in Israel. Scripture starts off telling us in Judges chapter 13, that again the Israelites did evil in the eyes of the Lord, so the Lord delivered them into the hands of the Philistines, for forty years. Forty is a number in scripture that represents deliverance. Whenever you see the number forty either someone is about to go into bondage or someone's coming out of bondage.

    After forty years an angel of the Lord appears to Samson's mother. Scripture never tell us her name all we know is that she is barren. The angel of the Lord tells her that although she is barren, she will have a son and that he will be called a Nazirite from his birth until the day of his death. He can never drink wine and he can never get a haircut. The angel tells Samson's parents that he will begin the deliverance of Israel from the hands of the Philistines.

I won't get into all the stories about Samson's mighty exploits, I do however, encourage you to read them for yourself. Samson kills many Philistines in his lifetime, and God uses this one man to be a perpetual thorn in the Philistine nation's side. Here's the problem with Samson. He's got really bad taste in women. They say you can't put a price on love but apparently, Delilah, the gold-digger Samson falls in love with can. She sells the secret of his strength to the Philistines for a promise of 1100 shekels of silver (from each Philistine ruler) about the equivalent of $275 US dollars. The Philistines capture him and gouge his eyes out.

Now as a parent, I can't help but read this story and cringe because Samson is living proof that the wrong woman or the wrong man, can cut your life off. Samson ruled twenty years, I believe he was supposed to rule for at least forty. But the wrong woman came into his life and derailed him from his destiny. Right now at the time of writing this book, my children, two boys and a girl, are 6, 9, and 12 years of age. I won't wait until they are twenty; I pray against the wrong man and the wrong woman for their lives now. If you are reading this and you have children, start doing that for your children as well. You may even want to start praying that for yourself. Pray for good friends and godly relationships because the right people can propel you towards the future God has in store for you, but the wrong people can pervert and destroy that future.

Samson is blind; he has no strength because the Spirit of the Lord God has left him. But he looks up to Heaven and he repents, and God alights upon him one more time, and Samson kills more Philistines in his death than he ever did alive.

SELAH NOTES

What news have you to report from the battle?
We have lost the battle to the Philistines, my lord. They are a powerful enemy.
How is this possible? Israel wins her battles because God fights for us!
Perhaps there is sin among us. Perhaps we should cry out to the Lord and repent.
Nonsense. We are better than those pagan Philistines! Send the Ark of the Covenant into the battle, then the Lord will have to fight for us.
SOON...

CHAPTER FIVE

THE PHILISTINES CAPTURE THE ARK

Now the Israelites went out to fight against the Philistines. The Israelites camped at Ebenezer, and the Philistines at Aphek. The Philistines deployed their forces to meet Israel, and as the battle spread, Israel was defeated by the Philistines, who killed about four thousand of them on the battlefield. When the soldiers returned to camp, the elders of Israel asked, "Why did the Lord bring defeat on us today before the Philistines? Let us bring the ark of the Lord's covenant from Shiloh, so that he may go with us and save us from the hand of our enemies." So the people sent men to Shiloh, and they brought back the ark of the covenant of the Lord Almighty, who is enthroned between the cherubim. And Eli's two sons, Hophni and Phinehas, were there with the ark of the covenant of God. When the ark of the

> **Israel always won their battles when they were faithful to God. Whenever there was sin in the camp they experienced defeat.**

Lord's covenant came into the camp, all Israel raised such a great shout that the ground shook. Hearing the uproar, the Philistines asked, "What's all this shouting in the Hebrew camp?" When they learned that the ark of the Lord had come into the camp, the Philistines were afraid. "A god has come into the camp," they said. "Oh no! Nothing like this has happened before. We're doomed! Who will deliver us from the hand of these mighty gods? They are the gods who struck the Egyptians with all kinds of plagues in the wilderness. Be strong, Philistines! Be men, or you will be subject to the Hebrews, as they have been to you. Be men, and fight!" So the Philistines fought, and the Israelites were defeated and every man fled to his tent. The slaughter was very great; Israel lost thirty thousand foot soldiers. The ark of God was captured, and Eli's two sons, Hophni and Phinehas, died. That same day a Benjamite ran from the battle line and went to Shiloh with his clothes torn and dust on his head. When he arrived, there was Eli sitting on his chair by the side of the road, watching, because his heart feared for the ark of God. When the man entered the town and told what had happened, the whole town sent up a cry. Eli heard the outcry and asked, "What is the meaning of this uproar?" The man hurried over to Eli, who was ninety-eight years old and whose eyes had failed so that he could not see. He told Eli, "I have just come from the battle line; I fled from it this very day." Eli asked, "What happened, my son?" The man who brought the news replied, "Israel fled before the Philistines, and the army has suffered heavy losses. Also your two sons, Hophni and Phinehas, are dead, and the ark of God has been captured." When he mentioned the ark of God, Eli *fell backward off his chair by the side of the gate. His neck was broken and he died, for he was an old man, and he was heavy. He had led Israel forty years. His daughter-in-law, the wife of Phinehas, was pregnant and near the time of delivery. When she heard the news that the ark of God had been captured and that her father-in-law and her husband were dead, she went into labor and gave birth, but was overcome by her labor pains. As she was dying, the women attending her said, "Don't despair; you have given birth to a son." But she did not respond or pay any attention. She named the boy Ichabod, saying, "The Glory has departed from Israel" — because of the capture of the ark of God and the deaths of her father-in-law and her husband. She said, "The Glory has departed from Israel, for the ark of God has been captured."*

1 Samuel 4:1-22

Eli is both high priest and judge, and he installs his two godless sons Hophni and Phinehas as priest. Israel's protector, Samson is gone, chopped down long before his prime, and now the Philistines are free to invade Israel again. Things aren't looking so good for the people of Israel, the Philistines are killing them by the thousands, and the elders began to ask the question, "Where is God? Why has He not given us the victory?"

Now you may remember that Israel always won their battles when they were faithful to God. Whenever there was sin in the camp they experienced defeat. Instead of the nation crying out to the Lord, and repenting before him, someone got the bright idea to bring the Ark of the Covenant into battle the next morning. They figured that if the Ark showed up then God would have to show up. If they brought His presence into the camp, God would surely route their enemies. So the two wicked sons of Eli dressed themselves in full priestly regalia and carried the ark into the battle. Eli's sons are killed, the ark is captured and it remains in Philistine territory for seven months. Seven is a number that represents completion. The Philistines set the Ark of the Covenant in the temple of their god Dagon and . . . oh boy, do I love this story! This is one of my absolute favorite stories in the Bible. Some people think that there is little value in reading the Old Testament. I believe just the opposite. It's when you read the Old Testament that you get to know God's personality and His nature. God really has a sense of humor. For seven months God inflicted the Philistines with tumors, diseases, boils, plagues and panic attacks. Some of you might not like the analogy I'm about to use for the King of Kings right now but God is straight up gangsta. In fact, He's the original gangsta. I'm not saying that God is a criminal. I'm using the word in a purely urban sense. If you still don't know what I mean. Keep reading and judge for yourself.   Watch what God does.

The Philistines believed that they could take God prisoner. So they set the Ark of the Covenant in Dagon's temple. They position the Ark so that it is seated before Dagon. As if to say, "Now the God of the Hebrews will answer to Dagon." The Lord breaks Dagon's hands, his feet and his neck. Then He makes the little statue bow before the Ark of the Covenant *in his own temple*. God's hand was so heavy upon the god Dagon and his people, that the Philistines started moving the Ark from town to town, city to city. The Philistines would see the Ark of the Covenant coming into their city they'd scream, "No! Send the God of Israel away from here or He will kill us!" So after seven months of this they had no other choice but to send the Ark back.

And so the God of Glory teaches everyone a lesson. He proves to both His people and His enemies that His presence can never be captured or contained, nor can He be manipulated or pimped. See, what'd I tell you? That's what you call straight up gangsta.

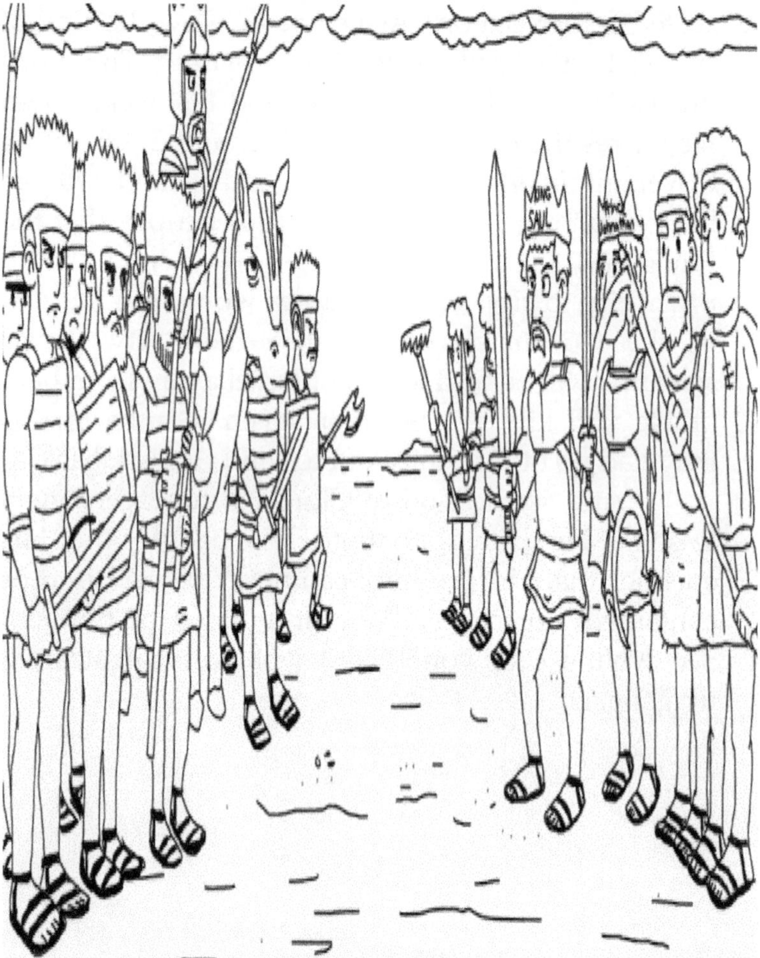
KING SAUL

CHAPTER SIX

A TECHNOLOGICALLY SUPERIOR ENEMY

Saul and his son Jonathan and the men with them were staying in Gibeah in Benjamin, while the Philistines camped at Mikmash. Raiding parties went out from the Philistine camp in three detachments. One turned toward Ophrah in the vicinity of Shual, another toward Beth Horon, and the third toward the borderland overlooking the Valley of Zeboyim facing the wilderness. Not a blacksmith could be found in the whole land of Israel, because the Philistines had said, "Otherwise the Hebrews will make swords or spears!" So all Israel went down to the Philistines to have their plow points, mattocks, axes and

> If the Philistines could have wiped Israel out they would have. If the devil that's hunting you could kill you, he would have done it already. He can't kill you because God is fighting for you. His only hope of destroying you is to get you to agree with death.

sickles sharpened. The price was two-thirds of a shekel for sharpening plow points and mattocks, and a third of a shekel for sharpening forks and axes and for repointing goads. So on the day of the battle not a soldier with Saul and Jonathan had a sword or spear in his hand; only Saul and his son Jonathan had them.

1 Samuel 13:16-22

The Philistines were educated. They were craftsmen and engineers by trade, they had impressive architecture, well fed horses, weapons of stone, chariots of iron. Israel on the other hand was a farming community. In fact, Israel had no army before the days of Saul. Saul instituted the first draft. Whenever war threatened the people of Israel they had to leave their fields to go fight. They didn't have horses, they had mules and oxen. They had plowshares, and pruning shears, all tools of a farmer.

To make matters worse, their oppressors, the Philistines, had outlawed blacksmiths in Israel, so the people had no means to fashion weapons of war during wartime. The whole army of three thousand fighting men owned two swords. The first belonged to the king, the other one belonged to his son, Jonathan.

Israel is literally outnumbered and out-gunned. Their fight is against an enemy who is not only technologically superior, but an enemy who has stripped them of their capacity to war. So the question that begs to be asked is this: if the Philistines were more numerous than Israel, and more technologically advanced than Israel, why did the Philistines feel the need to strip Israel of their capacity to war?

I believe the answer to this question lies in the fact that the Philistines had dealt with Israel many times before. Like any wise warrior they had studied their opponent. The Philistines had mixed it up with Israel enough times to know that even when victory appeared to be a sure thing, the Israelites still had an unfair advantage. You see, the God of the Hebrews was on their side. It didn't matter that Israel only had two swords because Israel received aid from a supernatural dimension.

I'll say it again, any worthy opponent will study his enemy. He will know his strengths as well as his weaknesses. In other words, he will be fully aware of his opponent's potential. Satan knows your potential. He has studied your family lineage for a very long time and he is a master at stealing your capacity to war.

He comes for our capacity to war because Satan knows that if you and I would just enter the battle as opposed to laying down and dying, taking whatever the enemy throws our way, if we would just mount up, then God would fight for us. Satan has read the script and he knows how this entire drama will unfold. He knows that the battle is not given to the swift or to the strong (him) but to the one who endures (you). So he comes to steal the very things that would help you to resist and endure.

Because Satan has read the script he comes after your joy. He has read the Word of God. The devil knows that God has given His followers a supernatural brand of joy. A Psalms 28:8 and a Nehemiah 8:10 kind of joy. It's the kind of joy that if those who love Him would just put a song of victory in their mouths God would endow them with courage and strength for the battle ahead. Satan knows that if you don't have joy you won't have the energy to resist, much less make war against him.

The enemy comes after your peace so that you won't be psychologically fit for battle. He sends a constant stream of haunting chatter to run through your mind like a freight train. So much so that you won't know where your thoughts end and his begins. Beloved, don't you know that the devil has read Matthew 8:24 and John 14:27? There is no way in hell that he wants you tapping into the supernatural brand of peace that Jesus left here on Earth for you. The kind of peace that allowed Jesus to be asleep on a boat in the middle of a ragging demonic storm. Nope, there is no way in hell he's going to sit by and just allow that. Satan could never break Jesus' peace, and he could never penetrate the fortress of our Savior's mind. You have both available to you. According to John 14:27 and Matthew 8:24 you have His peace, and according to the decree in Philippians 2:5 you can also have the mind of Christ.

Satan will shatter your unity with the people of God because he's read the Word of God that says a threefold cord is not easily broken (Ecclesiastes 4:12). He understands how math in God's kingdom works. He knows that just one puny human standing in agreement with God can put a thousand of his demonic troops to flight (Deuteronomy 32:30). Two puny humans standing together can put ten thousand of his demonic forces to flight. And just three, count them beloved, three mere mortals standing together trusting the Lord to work a miracle on their behalf, can put one hundred thousand demonic forces to flight. Are you kidding me? The devil can't have that. So every chance he gets he comes to steal your unity.

God knew that the battle would be mismatched; that's why He gave you these supernatural weapons in the first place. He has given us a whole arsenal of weapons that are not carnal but mighty through God for the purposes of pulling down strongholds (2 Corinthians 10:4). One of the most powerful weapons we have in that arsenal is God's name. In just a couple more chapters we will be talking about how to fight with the names of God but right now I want you to take a minute and focus on this one fact: **Israel only had two swords and the Philistines still couldn't wipe them out.**

So what does that say about the enemy that's raging against you? Newsflash folks, if the Philistines could have totally wiped Israel out they would have done it. And if the devil that's pursuing you could kill you, he would have done it by now. He can't kill you because God is fighting for you. Your enemy's only hope of destroying you is to get you to agree with death.

SELAH NOTES

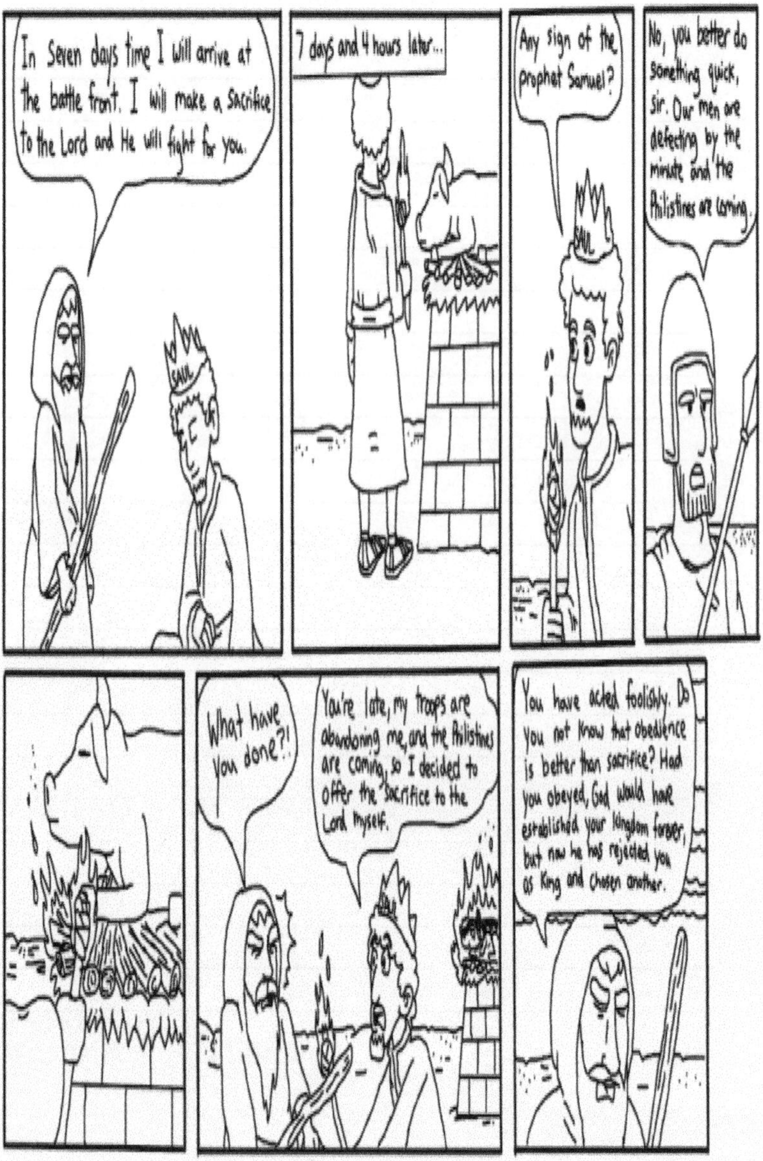

In Seven days time I will arrive at the battle front. I will make a Sacrifice to the Lord and He will fight for you.
7 days and 4 hours later...
Any sign of the prophet Samuel?
No, you better do something quick, sir. Our men are defecting by the minute and the Philistines are coming.
What have you done?!
You're late, my troops are abandoning me, and the Philistines are coming, so I decided to offer the Sacrifice to the Lord myself.
You have acted foolishly. Do you not know that obedience is better than sacrifice? Had you obeyed, God would have established your Kingdom forever, but now he has rejected you as King and chosen another.

CHAPTER SEVEN

KING SAUL WRITTEN OUT OF HISTORY

Saul was thirty years old when he became king, and he reigned over Israel forty-two years. Saul chose three thousand men from Israel; two thousand were with him at Mikmash and in the hill country of Bethel, and a thousand were with Jonathan at Gibeah in Benjamin. The rest of the men he sent back to their homes. Jonathan attacked the Philistine outpost at Geba, and the Philistines heard about it. Then Saul had the trumpet blown throughout the land and said, "Let the Hebrews hear!" So all Israel heard the news: "Saul has attacked the Philistine outpost, and now Israel has become obnoxious to the Philistines." And the

> The prince of the airwaves attacks you with climate. He charges the atmosphere with fear, and anxiety because he wants you to believe that he is so much bigger than what he really is. He wants you to do exactly what Israel did. Run for cover.

people were summoned to join Saul at Gilgal.

The Philistines assembled to fight Israel, with three thousand chariots, six thousand charioteers, and soldiers as numerous as the sand on the seashore. They went up and camped at Mikmash, east of Beth Aven. When the Israelites saw that their situation was critical and that their army was hard pressed, they hid in caves and thickets, among the rocks, and in pits and cisterns. Some Hebrews even crossed the Jordan to the land of Gad and Gilead.

Saul remained at Gilgal, and all the troops with him were quaking with fear. He waited seven days, the time set by Samuel; but Samuel did not come to Gilgal, and Saul's men began to scatter. So he said, "Bring me the burnt offering and the fellowship offerings." And Saul offered up the burnt offering. Just as he finished making the offering, Samuel arrived, and Saul went out to greet him.

"What have you done?" asked Samuel. Saul replied, "When I saw that the men were scattering, and that you did not come at the set time, and that the Philistines were assembling at Mikmash, I thought, 'Now the Philistines will come down against me at Gilgal, and I have not sought the Lord's favor.' So I felt compelled to offer the burnt offering."

"You have done a foolish thing," Samuel said. "You have not kept the command the Lord your God gave you; if you had, he would have established your kingdom over Israel for all time. But now your kingdom will not endure; the Lord has sought out a man after his own heart and appointed him ruler of his people, because you have not kept the Lord's command." Then Samuel left

Gilgal and went up to Gibeah in Benjamin, and Saul counted the men who were with him. They numbered about six hundred.
                                    1 Samuel 13:1-15

    Saul is the first king in Israel, and his first order of business is to institute a draft. He calls three thousand Israelite men into the army. He places two thousand troops under his command, and one thousand under his son Jonathan's command. Jonathan takes his thousand men and they attack a Philistine outpost. This time when the Philistines come to fight against Israel, they come fully locked and loaded. Three thousand chariots, six thousand charioteers, and soldiers as numerous as the sands on the sea shore and because Israel has initiated the attack, the Philistines are smoking mad.

    Historians and Bible scholars don't know what the Philistines actually called themselves. History only tells us what the Hebrews called them. The Hebrew word for Philistine means, to cover, to roll in on, to invade, and to divide. This gives us a picture of not only how the Philistine operated, but of the spiritual climate, and psychological terror they induced inside their adversaries as well.

    The enemy will attack you with climate. He is the prince of the airwaves so he charges the atmosphere with fear, and anxiety. He makes you think that he is so much bigger than what he actually is. He wants you to do exactly what Israel did. Run for cover, better yet join the other side.

"Don't try to fight against me it's pointless you can't win."

He is the master of smoke and mirrors, the ultimate king of mind trips. That's why the scripture says he is like a roaring lion. He magnifies himself. He's like the little man speaking through the voice distorter claiming to be the Great Wizard of Oz. Isaiah prophetically looking towards the end and to Satan's ultimate demise had this to say about him:

Those who see you stare at you, they ponder your fate: "Is this the man who shook the earth and made kingdoms tremble?"
Isaiah 14:16

The enemy who walks the earth seeking who he can devour will be, once revealed, unbelievably unremarkable.

Scripture says that when the men of Israel saw the Philistines lined up for battle, they realized that their situation was critical. Hello, can anybody say: two swords? Three thousand men and they only have two swords among them. Exactly how do you wage a war with two swords? Do you take turns with the swords? Pass them around? The Israelites began to dig holes in the ground and cover themselves with rocks. The army began to split up. Some of Israel's soldiers even defected to the Philistine side.

Saul sees his army dwindling, and he becomes afraid. Now Samuel who was prophet, priest, and judge of that day— the last judge to lead Israel, had already worked out the details with King Saul ahead of time. Samuel told Saul that in seven days he would arrive at the battle front, offer the sacrifice, say a few prayers and badda- bing- badda- boom, God would fight for Israel.

But the troops are scattering. It's past the seven-day mark and the prophet still hasn't showed up yet. Israel only has two swords. And Saul, because of his fear of this ancient enemy called the Philistines, is about to make the biggest mistake of his career. He calls for the sacrificial offering and sets it ablaze and greatly offends God. Samuel arrives, and rebukes Saul severely because at no time is a king ever to do the job of the priest. He tells him, "You have acted foolishly. You have not kept the command of the Lord. If you had, He would have established your kingdom over Israel forever. But now your kingdom will not endure. The Lord has sought out a man after His own heart and appointed him leader of His people in your place." We know that man to be David.

Let me interject a sidebar here and say that God is a God of the generations. When God cuts covenant with us He cuts covenant with everyone inside of us, because He is eternal and our lifespans are too short. Saul didn't understand this and so he will forevermore be listed in the history scrolls as the clinically depressed, psychotic king. While Jesus the Christ, the Lion of Judah, will enter the Earth heralded as the root and offspring of David.

So let me take a moment and sum up the history if I may. The Philistines have kidnapped grandma, killed Batman, captured the Ark of the Covenant, and took away Israel's ability to mass produce weapons of war. There's a freakishly large giant outside the camp taunting curses at them. God has rejected their king and they have two swords among them. Am I drawing the right picture for you? Now do you get it? Now do you see why a people with such a rich prophetic history could stand before this giant and be afraid? Scripture says this taunting and mocking went on for forty days. You may recall me saying earlier that forty is a number that represents deliverance. After forty days then came David.

SELAH NOTES

I admire your courage, David but you can't go out there. You are just a boy, and he is a man of war who has been fighting since youth. He will pulverize you
I killed both a lion and a bear, and with the help of the Lord I will cut down this uncircumcised Philistine too!
Go, and may the Lord be with you.
SO...
What?! Am I a dog that they send out a little boy to meet me? I will give your flesh to the birds of the air and the beasts of the field shall feast on your carcass tonight.
You come against me with a sword and a spear but I come against you with the name of the LORD!
Whir
whir
whir
Whizzz
AH!

CHAPTER EIGHT

THEN CAME DAVID

Now David was the son of an Ephrathite named Jesse, who was from Bethlehem in Judah. Jesse had eight sons, and in Saul's time he was very old. Jesse's three oldest sons had followed Saul to the war: The firstborn was Eliab; the second, Abinadab; and the third, Shammah. David was the youngest. The three oldest followed Saul, but David went back and forth from Saul to tend his father's sheep at Bethlehem. For forty days the Philistine came forward every morning and evening and took his stand. Now Jesse said to his son David, "Take this ephah of roasted grain and these ten loaves of bread for your brothers and hurry to their

> David, the man after God's heart, is the first person to bring the supernatural into the equation. David comes up with a different formula. A formula that has nothing to do with history and everything to do with who God is and Israel's relationship to Him.

camp. Take along these ten cheeses to the commander of their unit. See how your brothers are and bring back some assurance from them. They are with Saul and all the men of Israel in the Valley of Elah, fighting against the Philistines." Early in the morning David left the flock in the care of a shepherd, loaded up and set out, as Jesse had directed. He reached the camp as the army was going out to its battle positions, shouting the war cry. Israel and the Philistines were drawing up their lines facing each other. David left his things with the keeper of supplies, ran to the battle lines and asked his brothers how they were. As he was talking with them, Goliath, the Philistine champion from Gath, stepped out from his lines and shouted his usual defiance, and David heard it. Whenever the Israelites saw the man, they all fled from him in great fear. Now the Israelites had been saying, "Do you see how this man keeps coming out? He comes out to defy Israel. The king will give great wealth to the man who kills him. He will also give him his daughter in marriage and will exempt his family from taxes in Israel."

David asked the men standing near him, "What will be done for the man who kills this Philistine and removes this disgrace from Israel? Who is this uncircumcised Philistine that he should defy the armies of the living God?" They repeated to him what they had been saying and told him, "This is what will be done for the man who kills him." When Eliab, David's oldest brother, heard him speaking with the men, he burned with anger at him and asked, "Why have you come down here? And with whom did you leave those few sheep in the wilderness? I know how conceited you are and how wicked your heart is; you came down only to watch the battle." "Now what have I done?" said David. "Can't I even speak?" He then turned away to someone else and brought up the same matter, and the men answered him as before. What David said was overheard and reported to Saul, and Saul sent for him. David said to Saul, "Let no one lose heart on account of this Philistine; your servant will go and fight him." Saul replied, "You are not able to go out against this Philistine and fight him; you are only a young man, and he has been a warrior from his youth." But David said to Saul, "Your servant has been keeping his father's sheep. When a lion or a bear came and carried off a sheep from the flock, I went after it, struck it and rescued the sheep from its mouth. When it turned on me, I seized it by its hair, struck it and killed it. Your servant has killed both the lion and the bear; this uncircumcised Philistine will be like one of them, because he has defied the armies of the living God. The Lord who rescued me from the paw of the lion and the paw of the bear will rescue me from the hand of this Philistine. "Saul said to David, "Go, and the Lord be with you." Then Saul dressed David in his own tunic. He put a coat of armor on him and a bronze helmet on his head. David fastened on his sword over the tunic and tried walking around, because he was not used to them. "I cannot go in these," he said to Saul, "because I am not used to them." So he took them off. Then he took his staff in his hand, chose five smooth stones from the stream, put them in the pouch of his shepherd's bag and, with his sling in his hand, approached the Philistine.

    Meanwhile, the Philistine, with his shield bearer in front of him, kept coming closer to David. He looked

David over and saw that he was little more than a boy, glowing with health and handsome, and he despised him. He said to David, "Am I a dog that you come at me with sticks?" And the Philistine cursed David by his gods. "Come here," he said, "and I'll give your flesh to the birds and the wild animals!" David said to the Philistine, "You come against me with sword and spear and javelin, but I come against you in the name of the Lord Almighty, the God of the armies of Israel, whom you have defied. This day the Lord will deliver you into my hands, and I'll strike you down and cut off your head. This very day I will give the carcasses of the Philistine army to the birds and the wild animals, and the whole world will know that there is a God in Israel. All those gathered here will know that it is not by sword or spear that the Lord saves; for the battle is the Lord's, and he will give all of you into our hands." As the Philistine moved closer to attack him, David ran quickly toward the battle line to meet him. Reaching into his bag and taking out a stone, he slung it and struck the Philistine on the forehead. The stone sank into his forehead, and he fell face down on the ground. So David triumphed over the Philistine with a sling and a stone; without a sword in his hand he struck down the Philistine and killed him. David ran and stood over him. He took hold of the Philistine's sword and drew it from the sheath. After he killed him, he cut off his head with the sword.

When the Philistines saw that their hero was dead, they turned and ran. Then the men of Israel and Judah surged forward with a shout and pursued the Philistines to the entrance of Gath and to the gates of Ekron. Their dead were strewn along the Shaaraim road to Gath and Ekron. When the Israelites returned from chasing the Philistines, they plundered their camp. David took the Philistine's head and brought it to Jerusalem; he put the Philistine's weapons in his own tent. As Saul watched David going out to meet the Philistine, he said to Abner, commander of the army, "Abner, whose son is that young man?" Abner replied, "As surely as you live, Your Majesty, I don't know." The king said, "Find out whose son this young man is." As soon as David returned from killing the Philistine, Abner took him and brought him before Saul, with David still holding the Philistine's head. "Whose son are you, young man?" Saul asked him. David said, "I am the son of your servant Jesse of Bethlehem."

1 Samuel 17:12-58

Here's the thing you gotta love about David. We're in 1 Samuel chapter 17, but in the previous chapter David's been anointed by the prophet Samuel, as Israel's next King. He doesn't start ruling right away, he goes right back out into the sheep pen. Now scripture tells us a day is like a thousand years to God (2 Peter 3:8). Who knows what a chapter is like? We don't know how long it's been since David was anointed. It could be five years it could be ten, it could be just a matter of days. We simply don't know. What we do know is that David never complains.

Despise not the days of small beginnings. If a prophet comes and speaks an extraordinary word over your life, and you go right back to business as usually don't despair. Put your active agreement behind that prophetic word and watch God orchestrate destiny for you. I talk more about the concept of active agreement and the prophetic promise in my book *Wired for War*.

David's not complaining. He doesn't say, "God you said I'd be king, when will you keep your word to me?" No, he doesn't do anything like that. He goes back to his despised little sheep and he waits. David's brothers are off fighting in the war, so his father says, "Go take them some bread and find out how they are doing." David says, "No problem, happy to serve." He leaves his sheep in the care of a fellow shepherd, and heads out early that morning. David reaches the camp right about the time the troops were lining up to receive their daily verbal beat-down from Goliath.

David hears the giant's taunts, and a holy hatred rises up on the inside of him. David is standing on the precipice of destiny and he doesn't even know it. I want you to listen carefully to what David says. He says, "Who is this uncircumcised Philistine that he should defy the armies of the living God?"

Notice that David, the man after God's own heart, is the first person to bring the supernatural into the equation. This young man has "future king" written all over him. David starts doing some new math. He comes up with a completely different formula and it has nothing to do with Israel's historical backstory with the Philistines and everything to do with Israel's relationship to the Living God. David says, this giant is uncircumcised (outside the covenant). Plus, he's Philistine (an unbeliever). Plus, we are the army of Israel, multiply that by the fact that we belong to the Living God. David starts asking around. "What will king give the man who removes this disgrace from Israel?"

David's eldest brother Eliab, overhears David asking about the matter and the scripture says he burned with anger. Now remember, no one knows that David has been anointed to be the next King. No one except the Prophet Samuel, David, and David's family. Eliab who was passed over by God in favor of his youngest brother knows. Given his reaction towards David when he asks about Goliath we can deduce that older brother Eliab is still feeling mighty salty about little brother's prophecy. Eliab is what I call a Destiny Snatcher. These are people who are connected to you who are supposed to be for you but are secretly offended by the call of God on your life. Instead of helping you, instead of getting behind you and undergirding you, they try to use their rank and position in your life, to stop you from reaching your goals. Still when it comes time to seize your destiny you can't afford to be concerned about who is for you and who is not. You've got to keep moving and shake the haters off. Go ahead, pause for a moment and make a verbal declaration into the Earth about this.

Brother or not, Mother or not, when destiny calls, I will shake the haters off.

THE EARTH WILL HELP YOU

It doesn't matter who is against you, because the Earth will help you. David kills the giant with a rock, a piece of leather, and a stick. All articles from the Earth. People of God, I know it's a high thought but when it's time for you to step into your destiny, don't worry about who is with you or not. Don't concern yourself with what you have or don't have. *The Earth will help you.* Let me say it again. *The Earth will help you.* Okay, okay, maybe my way of saying this feels extra Biblical, or new age to you. Roman 8:19 says it like this: **all of creation is groaning, waiting in eager expectation for the manifestation of the sons of God.** And although it had not yet been written in the Earth at the time of its happening, Romans 8:19 is the reason the Red Sea parted so that the children of Israel could walk across on dry ground. Romans 8:19 is also the reason, why the water bowed to Peter when Jesus told him to get out the boat.

You might be thinking to yourself right about now, "Okay lady, you're kind of stretching it a bit here." But I tell you the truth, David caught the same revelation. That why he wrote the 98th psalm, where he declared:

Shout for joy to the Lord, all the earth. Let the sea resound, and everything in it. Let the rivers clap their hands, let the mountains sing together for joy; let them sing before the Lord, for he comes to judge the Earth.

The reason you picked up this book in the first place is because you heard that we would be studying the life of David. David was a master strategist who won every battle he ever fought. You want to learn how to win some battles of your own, so you might as well go ahead and catch the revelations that David caught. Even Jesus said it in the book of Luke, if they don't praise me the rocks will cry out (Luke 19:40). So don't tell me, that when you walk in your God given authority the Earth won't help you.

THE POWER OF THE TONGUE

Have you ever heard the turn of phrase, 'that person can talk a good game?' Well David talked a good game and God backed it up. There are no woof cookies being sold here. As soon as David speaks his words in the Earth realm, the giant drops dead in the spirit realm. Goliath is a dead man walking and he doesn't even know it! We know Goliath doesn't know it because he continues to mock Israel and their God. Perhaps if Goliath would have known in advance that the battle would have been so one-sidedly brutal and swift, he might have spent his last moments pleading for mercy. Let's play the footage back from the battle again, so we can take a closer look at what David said:

David said to the Philistine, "You come against me with sword and spear and javelin, but I come against you in the name of the Lord Almighty, the God of the armies of Israel, whom you have defied. This day the Lord will deliver you into my hands, and I'll strike you down and cut off your head. This very day I will give the carcasses of the Philistine army to the birds and the wild animals, and the whole world will know that there is a God in Israel. All those gathered here will know that it is not by sword or spear that the Lord saves; for the battle is the Lord's, and he will give all of you into our hands." As the Philistine moved closer to attack him, David ran quickly toward the battle line to meet him. Reaching into his bag and taking out a stone, he slung it and struck the Philistine on the forehead. The stone sank into his forehead, and he fell face down on the ground. So David triumphed over the Philistine with a sling and a stone; without a sword in his hand he struck down the Philistine and killed him.

1 Samuel 17:45-50

Did you catch that last part? Did you catch what the writer said in verse 50? Throughout this whole study we've been bemoaning the fact that Israel only has two swords and the writer of this passage makes it a point to say that David triumphs over the giant without the aid of a sword. Look at what David does. He lines up for battle, and he speaks to his enemy at the gate. I use this term gate metaphorically as an opening in time and space. David is speaking to the giant in the Valley of Elah, but in the realm of the Spirit, David is standing at a portal, an opening between Heaven and Earth. This is a spiritual gate. For a more in-depth discussion on the value and power of spiritual gates check out my book, *Intercession the Heartbeat of God*.

Because David is at the gate it's not just the giant, the Israelite army and the Philistine army that hear his words. The angelic forces both good and evil hear David's decree as well. If you read the above passage carefully you will see that David passes judgment on the giant before he ever even picks up a physical weapon. David passes judgment on the giant with his mouth. This is where the real battle is happening. David wars against the giant with the words that come out of his mouth. In the spirit realm, the moment David speaks, the giant falls over dead. The rock and the sling shot are for the live studio audience watching the battle on Earth. The rock and the sling shot were so that the people wouldn't think that by some sorcery the boy killed the giant. But make no mistake about it, God wanted this particular battle to be fought and won, with David's mouth.

David tells the giant you have defied the God of the armies of Israel. Why did David call God that? Why did he refer to God as the head of the army? Why didn't David say you have defied Jehovah Rohi, the Lord, my shepherd? The God who leads me beside still waters for His namesake. We know God certainly revealed Himself to David in this way, because David wrote the 23rd Psalm. Well the answer is simple. David wants and needs God to show up with a sword not a shepherd's staff. David wants and needs a military victory from God so he puts a demand on God's militaristic nature, the part of God that is a Man of War.

Beloved, can we talk candidly for a moment? Sometimes church folks can be . . . well you know, churchy. When we're in trouble we say idle little things like, "I just need God to show up and be God for me." Well what in the world does that mean? Telling God to be God to you is like asking gravity to hold you up. It's like asking to one day have death and to always taxes. These things already are. We have not because we ask not. And when we do muster up the courage to ask, we ask for the wrong things.

So come on, let's try this out. What is it that you need from God today? What aspect of His nature do you need to show up on your behalf? He is holding out his scepter to you. You have the Father's attention so go ahead and ask. And be specific.

You didn't press your way to the end of this book to leave without answers. Just like you don't press your way through the heavenly realm to stand before the King of Kings blubbering like someone who is outside of the covenant. Be like David and ask God for what you need.

"Lord I need you to be my provider. Or I need you to be a Man of War. Jesus my mind is racing a thousand miles per minute. I can't rest, I can't sleep, I can't think my way out of a paper bag right now, I need you to show yourself to me as the Prince of Peace." Isn't that so much better than God come and be God to me?

So my final question to you, before we finish our study is what are you speaking out of your own mouth? Maybe a better way to phrase that would be to ask, what battle are you currently losing that you could be winning with your mouth? Are you speaking words of victory, or words of sabotage?

All of heaven is standing at the gate waiting, to see what type of power will be released from your tongue. You've been silent for too long, it's time to open your mouth. Astound the devil, astound yourself. Call His name. Your help comes from the Lord.

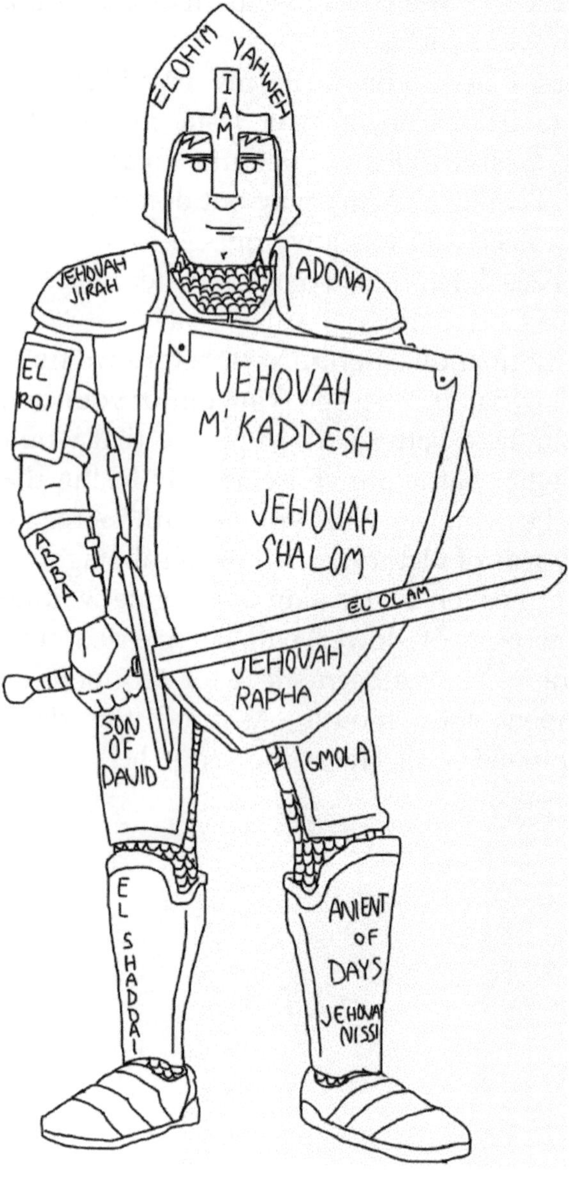
ELOHIM
YAHWEH
I AM
JEHOVAH JIRAH
ADONAI
EL ROI
JEHOVAH M'KADDESH
JEHOVAH SHALOM
ABBA
EL OLAM
JEHOVAH RAPHA
SON OF DAVID
GMOLA
EL SHADDAI
ANIENT OF DAYS
JEHOVA NISSI

CHAPTER NINE

GLOSSARY OF TERMS

TWENTY NAMES TO USE IN BATTLE

1. **Elohim:** When you call God Elohim you speak of His Power and His might. When the Earth was void and without form, it was the Spirit of Elohim that hovered over the face of the water. *It is he who made the earth by his power, who established the world by his wisdom, and by his understanding stretched out the heavens. Jeremiah 10:12*

   When to Use: Call on **Elohim** when you have a difficult matter to decipher. There is nothing He does not know. As Supreme Creator, He is the keeper of all wisdom and will gladly give to those who ask Him. Also call on **Elohim** when you are in need of the creative aspect of God's nature. As a writer, I call on the Spirit of **Elohim** to breathe on me and through me as I write my books.

2. **Adonai:** When you call God **Adonai** you recognize Him not only as your Lord but also as your master. As such He is owner of you and all

of your gifts, talents, and possessions. *Love the Lord your God and keep his requirements, his decrees, his laws and his commands always. Deuteronomy 11:1*

When to Use: For many of the people of God, Adonai will be a progression. When most believers are converted, they come to know God right away as Savior. He is **Yahweh the God who saves**. However, most new believers often do not operate or live in such a way that they owe their very allegiance to Him. Call on **Adonai** when you are ready to allow God to take you to this next level of service a place where your life is not your own. Where everything you are and everything you have belongs to Him. Just like salvation, you cannot accomplish this on your own. You need **Adonai** to make this radical conversion inside of you.

3. **I AM:** When you call God, **I AM** you understand that He has no beginning and He has no ending. He is constant and never changing. He can never be corrected or improved upon. He just is. When you call Him, **I AM** you recognize His utter supremacy. You recognize He is absolute reality and that everything that is not God remains in existence, moment by moment, only because God allows it. *Moses said to God, "Suppose I go to the Israelites and say to them, 'The God of your fathers has sent me to you,' and they ask*

me, 'What is his name?' Then what shall I tell them?" God said to Moses, "I AM WHO I AM. This is what you are to say to the Israelites: 'I AM has sent me to you.'" Exodus: 3:13-14

When to Use: Call on **I AM** when you need God to show up for you with the supremacy of His considerable force and His might. Also call on **I AM** when you need to remind yourself and every demonic force that's coming against you that your very existence (as well as the enemies) is rooted inside of the Great **I AM**. I like to call on the Great **I AM** often in times of high praise and worship when I am proclaiming or publishing His works throughout the Earth. I call on the Great **I AM** to honor and to bestow esteem upon God, to mock or reprimand His enemies, and to remind them of their eternal positioning beneath the Lord.

4. **Jehovah Mekaddishkem** (also spelled M'Kaddesh)**:** He is the God who sanctifies me. **Jehovah Mekaddishkem** makes me holy. *Say to the Israelites, 'You must observe my Sabbaths. This will be a sign between me and you for the generations to come, so you may know that I am the LORD, who makes you holy. Exodus 31:13*

When to Use: Call on the name of **Jehovah Mekaddishkem** when you need to be sanctified. We all are required to live a holy life, set apart for God, but like so many other things in this walk of faith, we cannot do it alone. Ask **Jehovah Mekaddishkem** to come and sanctify you, to sanctify you with fire from the inside out so that you may be holy and acceptable before Him, which is our reasonable service (Romans 12:1). There can be no true and lasting victory without sanctification. When the enemy comes for you, to sift you, you cannot have his stuff. You must be free of his sin: his pride, his lust, his fear, his rage. **Jehovah Mekaddishkem** will come into your life if you ask Him to and burn these things out.

5. **Jehovah Rohi:** The Lord my shepherd. This is the God David discovered when he was out in the desert tending his father's sheep. *The LORD is my shepherd, I lack nothing. He makes me lie down in green pastures, he leads me beside quiet waters, he refreshes my soul. He guides me along the right paths for his name's sake. Even though I walk through the darkest valley, I will fear no evil, for you are with me; your rod and your staff, they comfort me You prepare a table before me in the presence of my enemies. You anoint my head with oil; my cup overflows. Surely your goodness and love will follow me all the days of my life, and I will dwell in the house of the LORD forever. Psalms 23*

When to Use: Call on **Jehovah Rohi** when you need guidance, refreshing, inner peace, and courage to walk through a difficult or fearful place. Call on **Jehovah Rohi** when you feel weak and tired from a spiritual or emotional battle. Call on **Jehovah Rohi** when you need your spiritual hearing fine-tuned. There are many voices speaking in the spirit realm, many of these voices are louder than God's. It is Jesus as **Jehovah Rohi** who declares that His sheep know His voice and another they will not follow. Also call on **Jehovah Rohi** when you realize or think that you may have been led astray or duped by false teachers or occultist leaders. Cry out to **Jehovah Rohi** and He will quickly come find you and gently guide you back to the right path with His shepherd's hook.

6. **Jehovah Shammah:** God is present. Jehovah is there. *God is our refuge and strength, a very present help in trouble. Psalm 46:1*

    When to Use: Call on **Jehovah Shammah** when you have trouble staying in the right now, if you are tormented with scenes from your past, or obsessed with thoughts, hopes or dreams and desires for the future, call on **Jehovah Shammah** and know that the power of God is available for you right in the here and now, today. The healing that **Jehovah Shammah** offers you today is the only way to escape the torment of the past and it's the only way to get to the future you are destined for. Also call on **Jehovah Shammah** if you are tormented by feelings of loneliness, isolation, fear, helplessness, and depression. If you call to Him, **Jehovah Shammah** will come to your aid and He will provide refuge from every demonic storm.

7. **Jehovah Rapha:** The Lord your God is your healer. *I will exalt you, Lord, for you lifted me out of the depths and did not let my enemies gloat over me. Lord my God, I called to you for help, and you healed me. You, Lord, brought me up from the realm of the dead; you spared me from going down to the pit. Psalm 30:1-3*

    When to Use: When you stand on the name of **Jehovah Rapha** you are recognizing that not only is God a healer, which, for most believers, that is the easy part. We know God heals. We've read the Bible stories and heard the amazing testimonies of all the many times **Jehovah Rapha** showed up and either healed or raised the dead. Where modern day Christians tend to struggle is in seeing so much premature death and disease in the world today, especially among believers. We know that God is a healer but we don't always believe that He wants to heal or that He is willing to heal. I encourage you to call on **Jehovah Rapha** if this is your struggle. God always wants to heal. Healing is His will if it were not so, then Christ would not have born the weight of our infirmities: sin, disease, and death in his physical body. Healing, as well as the ability to raise the dead, are a part of our divine spiritual inheritance. The infant church was born doing these things: healing the sick, raising the dead and casting out demons — all forms of healing. When you call on **Jehovah Rapha** you pull on that aspect of God's divine nature that **wants** to heal both you and others, your body, mind, and spirit. When you call on **Jehovah Rapha** you put a demand on healing. Call on **Jehovah Rapha** when you need sickness cured and the dead raised.

8. **Jehovah Tsidkenu:** The Lord our righteousness. *"The days are coming," declares the Lord, "when I will raise up for David a righteous Branch, a King who will reign wisely and do what is just and right in the land. In his days Judah will be saved and Israel will live in safety. This is the name by which he will be called: The Lord Our Righteous Savior. Jeremiah 23: 5-6*

When to Use: Call on the name of **Jehovah Tsidkenu** when the enemies of doubt, fear, regret, guilt and confusion come to convince you of your unrighteousness. These particular spirits often attack believers during times of praise and worship when it is time to lift your voice in a corporate setting to exalt and welcome in the Lord as King. These spirits come to convince believers of their unrighteousness. In those times the people of God should agree with the adversary quickly, "Yes, you are right, devil, I am not righteous in and of myself." Then call on the name of **Jehovah Tsidkenu**. "But I thank God that the Branch, Jesus, **Jehovah Tsidkenu** made me righteous." If you have unrepentant sin in your life repent, but do not allow the enemy to torment you with the charge of unrighteousness. None are righteous that's why we need Jesus. Also call on the name of **Jehovah Tsidkenu** when people rise up and make false claims against you and you need the justice of your cause to shine bright like the noonday sun.

9. **Jehovah Jireh:** Jehovah will see to it. The Lord will provide. *Then God said, "Take your son, your only son, whom you love – Isaac – and go to the region of Moriah. Sacrifice him there as a burnt offering on a mountain I will show you." Early the next morning Abraham got up and loaded his donkey. He took with him two of his servants and his son Isaac. When he had cut enough wood for the burnt offering, he set out for the place God had told him about. On the third day Abraham looked up and saw the place in the distance. He said to his servants, "Stay here with the donkey while I and the boy go over there. We will worship and then we will come back to you." Abraham took the wood for the burnt offering and placed it on his son Isaac, and he himself carried the fire and the knife. As the two of them went*

on together, Isaac spoke up and said to his father Abraham, "Father?" "Yes, my son?" Abraham replied. "The fire and wood are here," Isaac said, "but where is the lamb for the burnt offering?" Abraham answered, "God himself will provide the lamb for the burnt offering, my son." And the two of them went on together. When they reached the place God had told him about, Abraham built an altar there and arranged the wood on it. He bound his son Isaac and laid him on the altar, on top of the wood. Then he reached out his hand and took the knife to slay his son. But the angel of the Lord called out to him from heaven, "Abraham! Abraham!" "Here I am," he replied. "Do not lay a hand on the boy," he said. "Do not do anything to him. Now I know that you fear God, because you have not withheld from me your son, your only son." Abraham looked up and there in a thicket he saw a ram caught by its horns. He went over and took the ram and sacrificed it as a burnt offering instead of his son. So Abraham called that place The Lord Will Provide. And to this day it is said, "On the mountain of the Lord it will be provided." Genesis 22: 2-14

When to Use: Call on the name of **Jehovah Jireh,** when you need God to provide both the seed and the harvest for the impossible thing that He Himself has promised you. Just as it was physically impossible to Abraham to have a son by his wife, Sarah, the son that God promised. **Jehovah Jireh** wants to blow your mind and provide the very thing for you that you believe is impossible to happen. The **Jireh,** aspect of Jehovah's nature demands that He both provide the promise AND protect the promise, to see it to fruition. **Jehovah will see to it.** Just as He protected Abraham's promised son Isaac. Call on **Jehovah Jireh** when you need help believing God to provide the vision. Call on **Jehovah Jireh** when you need help and fortification to stay faithful and true to God once the promise arrives so that the promise does not become an idol in your heart. Also call on **Jehovah Jireh** to protect every aspect of the developing promise. Parents should call on **Jehovah Jireh** to oversee the development, care and the futures of their children.

10. Jehovah Nissi: The Lord Is my Banner. When the enemy comes in on the people of God like a flood, **Jehovah Nissi** raises up a banner. *Moses said to Joshua, "Choose some of our men and go out to fight the Amalekites. Tomorrow I will stand on top of the hill with the staff of God in my hands. So Joshua fought the Amalekites as Moses had ordered, and Moses, Aaron and Hur went to the top of the hill. As long as Moses held up his hands, the Israelites were winning, but whenever he lowered his hands, the Amalekites were winning. When Moses' hands grew tired, they took a stone and put it under him and he sat on it. Aaron and Hur held his hands up — one on one side, one on the other — so that his hands remained steady till sunset. So Joshua overcame the*

Amalekite army with the sword. Then the Lord said to Moses, "Write this on a scroll as something to be remembered and make sure that Joshua hears it, because I will completely blot out the name of Amalek from under heaven." Moses built an altar and called it The Lord is my Banner. Exodus 17: 8-15

When to Use: We access this aspect of God's nature, **Jehovah Nissi**, when we praise Him. Begin to celebrate **Jehovah Nissi** BEFORE the battle is over. When you see even a tiny bit of evidence in the Earth of God fighting for or working a situation out for your good, begin to praise **Jehovah Nissi** like you've lost your mind. Praise Him like Publishers Clearing House just rang your doorbell and presented you with a 40 million dollar check. Just as Moses kept his arms up during the battle, when you praise **Jehovah Nissi** in the midst of the battle you ensure your victory. After all, no one brings out their victory banners when they think they are going to be beaten. Banners are for celebration. We celebrate before the battle is won because we trust **Jehovah Nissi,** our banner, for the outcome.

11. **Jehovah Shalom: The Lord Is My Peace** *I have told you these things, so that in me you may have peace. In this world you will have trouble. But take heart! I have overcome the world." John 16:33*

When to Use: Jehovah Shalom represents the aspect of His nature that Jesus promised us. Jesus tells us clearly that His peace is not like the world's peace. In the world, peace means the cessation of war. **Jehovah Shalom** will grant you peace whether the battle rages or not. When you call on **Jehovah Shalom** you will be able to rest peacefully in the most adverse conditions of life. Call on **Jehovah Shalom** if you suffer from sleep disorders such as insomnia, anxiety disorders and hypertension and also suffer from hearing multiple voices, and mind chatter.

12. **Jehovah Sabaoth: The Lord of Hosts**. The Lord of armies. The Lord of powers. The name **Jehovah Sabaoth** denotes God's universal sovereignty over every militaristic force both in the spiritual realm and in the temporal realm. **Jehovah Sabaoth** is the King of all of Heaven and Earth. *Do you think I cannot call on my Father and he will at once put at my disposal more than twelve legions of angels? Matthew 26:53*

When to Use: Just because He is God all by Himself does not mean He is by Himself. Every power in existence must bow before **Jehovah Sabaoth**. Call on **Jehovah Sabaoth** when you feel like the enemy has you backed into a corner and surrounded on every side. Call on **Jehovah Sabaoth** to remind yourself that there are always more for you then those who are against you. Call on **Jehovah Sabaoth** when you need God to release warring angels to accomplish any God given task.

13. **EL Gmolah: The God of Recompense or Reward**. The Lord of retribution. *Men do not despise a thief, if he steals to satisfy his soul when he is hungry; but if he be found, he shall restore sevenfold, he shall give all the substance in his house. Proverbs 6:30-31*

The great civil rights activist and abolitionist Harriet Tubman was a prophet who knew this aspect of God's nature, **EL Gmolah,** the God of recompense. While she was yet a slave, Harriet Tubman, secured the services of a lawyer who did some digging around only to discover that Harriet's mother's freedom had been stolen by her current master. This master for the sake of his own greed had not followed the dictates of a previous owner's will and set Harriet's mother free upon his death. As a result, not only was Harriet's mother's freedom stolen, because the laws in the south at that time declared that the children followed the condition of the mother, Harriet and all of her siblings' freedom was stolen too. Harriet said that she hated this man when she had found out what he had done to her family, until the Lord spoke to her and told her not to hate this man, but instead to pray for him daily. Harriet prayed for her master every day and God birthed forgiveness for that man inside of Harriet's soul. According to the scripture in Proverbs 6, Harriet recognized the thief; she took this man before **El Gmolah**. The wicked master died mysteriously and painfully **and El Gmolah** recompensed Harriet Tubman many more lives for the lives of herself and her family members that had been stolen. She made 19 trips into the south, escorted over 300 slaves to freedom and never once lost a passenger on the Underground Railroad.

When to Use: It is very common for the people of God to become bitter when they are treated unjustly particularly around areas of racial injustice. Instead of becoming bitter, call on **El Gmolah** when you recognize a thief that has stolen from you, your family line, your community and or your ancestors.

14. **El ElYON: The Most High God.** *The Son is the image of the invisible God, the firstborn over all creation. For in him all things were created: things in heaven and on earth, visible and invisible, whether thrones or powers or rulers or authorities; all things have been created through him and for him. He is before all things, and in him all things hold together Colossians 1: 15-17*

When to Use: When the enemy is standing flat footed in your face telling you what he is about to do to you. You just remember he works for **El ElYON** and that he can do nothing to you except **El ElYON** allows it.

15. **El Roi**: The strong God who **sees me**. *The angel of the LORD found Hagar near a spring in the desert; it was the spring that is beside the road to Shur. And he said, "Hagar, slave of Sarai, where have you come from, and where are you going?" "I'm running away from my mistress Sarai," she answered. Then the angel of the LORD told her, "Go back to your mistress and submit to her." The angel added, "I will increase your descendants so much that they will be too numerous to count." The angel of the LORD also said to her: "You are now pregnant and you will give birth to a son. You shall name him Ishmael, for the LORD has heard of your misery. He will be a wild donkey of a man; his hand will be against everyone and everyone's hand against him, and he will live in hostility toward all his brothers." She gave this name to the LORD who spoke to her: "You are the God who sees me," for she said, "I have now seen the One who sees me." Genesis 16:7-13*

Hagar was just a slave girl, an invisible single mother, caught up in some other folk's family drama. When she fled to the desert and decided she would die the Lord appeared to her and she called him **El Roi** the strong one who sees me.

When to Use: Call on **El Roi** when you feel invisible. When you are in need of revelation concerning your future call on **El Roi**. When you have trouble seeing who you really are in Christ, or the future He has for you, call on **El Roi**. When dealing with oppressive leadership or corrupt government cry out to **El Roi**.

16. **El Shaddai:** The all-sufficient one, the multi breasted one. All sufficient, All bountiful. He can sustain you and me, and everybody else all at the same time. *When Abram was ninety-nine years old, the LORD appeared to him and said, "I am God Almighty; walk before me faithfully and be blameless. Then I will make my covenant between me and you and will greatly increase your numbers." Genesis 17:1-2*

    When to Use: Call on **El Shaddai** when you need an increase of God's power, love, infilling, and provision present in your life.

17. **El Olam:** The Everlasting God. *Do you not know? Have you not heard? The Everlasting God, the LORD, the Creator of the ends of the earth does not become weary or tired. His understanding is inscrutable. He gives strength to the weary, And to him who lacks might He increases power. Isaiah 40: 28-29*

When to Use: There are times as believers when we feel like we just can't last. Call on **El Olam** when you need endurance. When you feel tired. Call on **EL Olam** to help you resist temptation. He will grant you with the strength to endure.

18. **Ancient of Days:** The God who existed before days began. *"As I looked, "thrones were set in place, and the Ancient of Days took his seat. His clothing was as white as snow; the hair of his head was white like wool. His throne was flaming with fire, and its wheels were all ablaze. A river of fire was flowing, coming out from before him. Thousands upon thousands attended him; ten thousand times ten thousand stood before him. The court was seated, and the books were opened. Daniel 7:9-10.*

    When to Use: When you are faced with an overwhelming trial call on the **Ancient of Days**, when you are coming up against powers, thrones, dominions, and principalities call on the **Ancient of Days**. It doesn't matter how big the devil that's coming against you is, how long he's been around, I promise you he's a preschooler compared to your God because you serve the **Ancient of Days.**

19. **He's the Intercessor and the Amen:** The God who prays and the God who answers. *In the same way the Spirit also helps our weakness; for we do not know how to pray as we should, but the Spirit*

Himself intercedes for us with groaning too deep for words; and He who searches the hearts knows what the mind of the Spirit is, because He intercedes for the saints according to the will of God. Romans 8:26-27

Jesus, on the other hand, because He continues forever, holds His priesthood permanently. Therefore He is able also to save forever those who draw near to God through Him, since He always lives to make intercession for them. Hebrews 7:24-25

He prays the prayer and He answers the prayer. Wow! That's Amazing. The God we serve is truly amazing. He is the **Intercessor and the Amen**. That means His Spirit prays the prayer through you, and then He is the one who stamps, "Amen, so be it." on the prayer when it's done. If we understood this aspect of God's nature we'd be more likely to pray. We'd be less likely to let the enemy convince us that our prayers are ineffectual or just wrong. In fact, in the book of Revelation Jesus calls Himself the **Amen**. *To the angel of the church in Laodicea write: The Amen, the faithful and true Witness, the Beginning of the creation of God. Revelation 3:14*

When to Use: Call on the **Intercessor and the Amen** when you think your prayers aren't effective.

***20.* Abba:** Daddy God, Father, Source. *The Spirit you received does not make you slaves, so that you live in fear again; rather, the Spirit you received brought about your adoption to sonship. And by him we cry, "Abba, Father." Romans 8:15*

When to Use: When all else fails, when my heart becomes full and I run out of fancy words to say, and I can't remember any other name, I let the tears spill down my face and I cry **Abba!** Daddy, please come see about me. Any parent knows a child in distress can get a lot of mileage just by simply screaming one word, "Daddy!" If you are a parent and you hear your child cry like this, you will leap tall buildings in a single bound. You will run through hell and high water, or at least die trying just to get to them. If we are only lumps of clay and we know how to do right, what more will our **Abba,** Daddy do? Will He not send help from His sanctuary when you call?

EPILOGUE

AN INVITATION TO JOIN THE FAMILY OF GOD

If you're reading this book and you've never made a commitment to Jesus Christ, I'd like to introduce you right now to Yahweh the God who saves. I invite you now to make Jesus the Savior of your life. Salvation is truly where this journey begins. If you would like the Lord Jesus to come and live in your heart, simply pray the following prayer:

Lord Jesus,

I believe you and I believe in you. I believe you are the Word made flesh who came to live among humans. I believe that not only are you the son of the Living God, You are God. I acknowledge that the only path to eternal life for me is through You. I believe that you came to Earth, lived and died as a man to save me from the penalty of sin and death. So Lord Jesus, I receive your perfect gift of salvation. I receive you as my Savior, I ask that you come into my heart and become my friend, my Master and My Lord. Live inside of me forevermore. In your name, Jesus I pray. Amen.

Beloved, if you prayed that prayer, not just merely read the words on the page, but if you prayed it and you meant it in your heart then you've just been born again. Right now the angels in Heaven are rejoicing over you. You see they understand something that I pray you will one day understand too— if no one else ever on the planet would have accepted the precious gift of salvation, Jesus would have still shed His divinity, come to the Earth as a man, lived for 33 ½ years, and died—just for you. Welcome to the kingdom, beloved. Salvation is foyer. Enter in to so much more.

Dear Reader,

I hope you've enjoyed, *Doing Battle with the Names of God Spiritual Warfare for the Reluctant Warrior.* If you have been blessed by this book please, go online and spread the good news. Write a Facebook post, tweet about it, most importantly you can write a review. You can place that review on Amazon, Goodreads, or whatever forum you typically purchase books from. Customers often think that their reviews hold little value, however reviews go a long way in helping authors, especially independent authors such as myself reach more people for the kingdom. Your review doesn't have to be long, it doesn't have to be eloquent, it only needs to be honest and from the heart. Also, I love to hear from my readers so if you have any questions about the material presented in this book, or you just want to drop me a line to say hello, you can contact me at **doingbusiness withgod@gmail.com**. Until we meet again, blessing to you and your house.

Sincerely,

Catrina J. Sparkman

ABOUT THE AUTHOR

Catrina J. Sparkman is a licensed, ordained minister and the founder of The Ironer's Press Ministries, which hosts Prayer Parties— a seasonal gathering of intercessors from all over the Midwest, as well as The Fourth Watch— a 3-6am prayer meeting, that happens every Friday morning in her home city. She is the author of various works of fiction and non-fiction. An inspirational speaker, consultant, presenter, and personal empowerment coach, for various churches and secular organizations, Catrina teaches on prayer, the prophetic ministry, healing and deliverance, and theatre arts. Mrs. Sparkman lives in Madison, WI with her husband, Wesley, and their three beautiful children. She can be reached at **doingbusinesswithgod@gmail.com**.

BOOKING INFO

To book Minster Sparkman for your next ministry event please contact: Kubernesis Administrative Services on behalf of the Ironer's Press. T: 858 663.7810 **kubernesis.info@gmail.com**